IN OUR BEAUTIFUL BONES

IN OUR BEAUTIFUL BONES

Poems
by Zilka Joseph

Mayapple Press 2021

Published by   Mayapple Press
                 362 Chestnut Hill Road
                 Woodstock, NY 12498
                 mayapplepress.com

ISBN 978-1-952781-07-0
Library of Congress Control Number 2021943102

Gratitude

Many thanks to Judith Kerman. For your strong and adventurous spirit, your important contributions to publishing for so many years, and for your whole-hearted support of this book.

Thanks to Sharon Backstrom, who (along with my friend, late Nancy Williams), has always rooted for me and my poetry. Thanks for your encouragement and for sponsoring the artwork for my book cover.

Thank you, Rowe Lee-Mills, for your kindness and support.

Maria Mazzioti Gillan, Diane Seuss, Sumita Charkarborty, Desiree Cooper, Lolita Hernandez, and Kirun Kapur, all brilliant writers whom I look up to. Thanks for your generosity and for taking the time to endorse my work.

Thanks to artist and fellow Bene Israel, Siona Benjamin, for allowing me to use your gorgeous painting for my cover. www.artsiona.com

My thanks to John. You are my heart and my home.

Cover art:
Exodus #2, 21" x 16" gouache, 22K gold leaf and mixed media on museum board mounted on wood panel.
Artist: © Siona Benjamin 2016.
Website: *www.artsiona.com*

Photo of author by John Joseph. Book and cover designed by Judith Kerman with text and titles in Adobe Caslon Pro.

Contents

Always, for John.

For oppressed and persecuted people everywhere,

and for those who speak truth to power.

and they resume their journey
flying by night
with the sound
of blood rushing in an ear

—"Migration," W.S. Merwin

An immigrant is a kind of suicide.
(Sonnet 27)

—"White Elephants," Reetika Vazirani

Which language
has not been the oppressor's tongue?
Which language
truly meant to murder someone?

—"A Different History," Sujata Bhatt

God bless
every beautiful thing
called monstrous
since the dawn
of a colonizer's time.

—"Benediction," Joshua Bennet

Voyage

—The Upanishads explain how wisdom can be absorbed through sound, how the ear is a vessel—the receiver of divine messages

The lightning fell, and I only knew

that it entered my eyes, and thunder
repeated words in my ears
I could not understand

in the grey-blue light of evening.
A sheet of silver drew itself
like a shroud over my car—

its engine an animal thrashing
in the hold, my heartbeat
like oars slamming hard

against every climbing wave,
my hands on the steering wheel
clawing at it as if it were

a raft. At sixteen, my father sailed
the Bombay steamships, nearly
deafened by their sound;

gales, ice, St. Elmo's fire striking
on the high seas, then sailed diesel
vessels through squalls

when the sky was black and the water
black, and the sailor's hearts
shrunk from fear—

all listening, on deck and on the bridge
and in the bowels
of the engine room,

to what the thunder said. And turning
into a vacant lot on Opdyke
near Pontiac, the storm

washed me clean
off the road. Wipers swept leaves
and yellow-black sky into sea

foam. I watched the windshield bulge
like a goatskin. It strained,
but held. Then a dam of white

light broke, the wall of water
shattering its cargo, and me
inside it like a seed

giving itself up to water
and to wind. In the west,
the sunlight crashing

in the broken branches
of oaks, burned a tunnel
of sienna through

which the bow
of my ship rose
to meet the horizon,

and my father, the Chief,
roared to his engineers,
their faces streaked with oil

and boiler suits sweat drenched;
men whose torn lips
bled as another peal shook

the flailing vessel, and we turned
our faces to the upper
deck. Like our Jewish

ancestors wrecked on the
Konkan coast thousands
of years ago, we waited

but no calm came
until the wind suddenly
fell. My car almost shoved

on to its side, now only swayed,
a metal cradle
spat from the mouth

of thunder. I smelled its breath,

its teeth left bloodless marks
on my skin, my bones
shook, and though it was gone

I felt its pull, a lift,
a nameless terror,
and my deafened ears

received every word it said—
what it had said
to my ancestors

what it had said
to my father
to his men

as it had let the sailors go,
as it had let my father go
and let us all go home.

1

Drinking Vodka at 35,000 ft.

I ask for vodka and orange, speak clearly
so the hostess won't have to ask me again,
am conscious of her tall figure as she jokes
with passengers, laughs so easily
I envy her, suddenly feel the jab
of the arm of the giant man
crammed into the economy

seat beside me. His pudgy fingers
pass me the small plastic glass
and tiny bottles, the *Absolut* winks,
the orange juice and pretzels
follow. I thank him, he smiles, he's chosen
vodka too. *I'm from Peoria*, he says,

and before I can ask where that is,
says *I'm traveling back from Perth.*
I can't imagine how he survived, trapped
in a small seat half his size. I think of Alice
in Wonderland growing and growing
till she breaks through the roof,
the walls, the windows. *I'm from Calcutta,*

I say, *joining my husband in Chicago…*
I've never drunk vodka so high in the air.
One sip and I think—Am I drunk—
are my words slurring? I sip slowly,
my tongue plays with the ice,
and I watch the TV monitor showing
where the aircraft is at this moment,
the names of mountain ranges, lakes,
snow-capped peaks we fly over,

and when we cross Dover I notice
frilly waves frozen along the shore,
sigh when the arrow points to Cork
where a 747 crashed some years ago.
Will I see my parents again?

The hostess brings strange lunch—
strong smelling salmon with sour cream,
a spiky salad. I am already full with too-tart
orange juice, but a gentle vodka-and-sun
buzz soothes me. The bitter taste of the transit
at Frankfurt leaves me slowly. The tall officers
in black uniforms with piercing ice-blue
eyes, some staring, some following
the sleepy, confused passengers,
their black and tan German Shepherds
sniffing the legs, bags, purses
of frightened women and children
as they passed. I finish my drink,

my fingers cold. Wildfire panic
flaring at the thought of crossing
this threshold, and immigration officers
who'll grill me with questions. How
will I answer through this haze,
this heaviness, this pain
I have never felt before.
Is this is what people call jetlag?
Homesickness? I fall into half

sleep, my body numb. The man from Peoria
stirs in his seat, a fold of fat from his belly
slips along the hand-rest separating us
and pushes up against my arm
which falls as his elbow
shoves mine in sleep, his body

slumped, his head lolling. I guess the vodka
worked nicely for him. The plane banks
left, then right, we wake, my stomach
lurches. The seat belt sign comes on,
the funny hostess leans over
to check on us. Is my husband
really waiting for me? This distance

has grown dangerous. We look
out the window. The man from Peoria

points to some tall needly black buildings
stabbing the blue sky below—
Downtown Chicago, he says,
wow, I say, but I have no clue
what downtown means,

he says *Look what a beautiful day it is!*
The lake is so blue, a blue I've never seen before,

I search my "English teacher" vocabulary
for a perfect image, just the right fit—
hmm maybe *forget-me-not blue?*
Lake Michigan spreading below
is a vast bright sea,
and there are tiny white boats
like stitches all over it;
the sky is full of still-life
airplanes, suspended
at different levels, hanging

in cobalt air. I cry at the beauty.
But I think of Dante's *Purgatorio*—
the tiered stages, the tortured souls
circling the spirals,
and our aircraft glides
down, down, down.

Introduction to Circles

Perhaps I was confused

by the arched glass of Sears Tower,
the silver El winding the loop, its roar
echoing in the canyons of buildings,
the whine of the saxophone
scraping Saks' rotating doors, and the low
growls from the bearded man,
his legless body in fatigues,
selling flags

by American Girl Place. Maybe I was dizzy

because while looking for the bus stop for the 145
I wandered into a circle of people
screaming *don't buy fur, don't kill*
the animals just outside Marshal Fields
on Michigan Avenue. So when Martha
asked me to join her book club,
a group of fortyish women, with high-
profile careers, all big business school
alumna, I was overwhelmed by her kindness,
thinking it would be great to make
friends, treat myself to intellectual
discussion. They had chosen Arundhati Ray's
The God of Small Things and thought I could

tell them about India. It was strange

hearing the names of the characters
from their mouths. *How come* they asked me
you speak such good English?
Then asked about arranged marriage.
Told me later, of course, I knew, didn't I
that they were all divorced? And now dating
furiously, and finding only frogs? No princes,
even in Europe where they traveled for business.
Maria told me she had immersed

herself in the Japanese language
and culture, because her ex was
Japanese, but being Catholic refused
to give her a divorce. Nancy said she married
a man from Norway but living there
depressed her, so they moved here,
and he looked for a job, but wasn't happy.
Killed himself while she was at work,
showed me where she had found him
when she came home. As I listen

I feel the pin-pricks of curious eyes, an unspoken
rush of questions they're too polite to ask but finally do—
about the oppression of women,
about my being a professional
but barred from working for five years,
and the fact that I'm "still" married. I find it hard
to answer, eat, and while eating talk
about the caste system,

the status of women—or the lack of it, terrified

of dropping crumbs or spilling my wine, all the while
explaining behavioral patterns and traditions
of life forms on my planet. They ask me
to pick a book for next time. I choose
Song of Solomon. They have barely heard
of it. Two of them say they've seen Toni Morrison
on the Oprah show, and then ask,
you do see Oprah there? Is this how
an ambassador feels? At least

diplomats are groomed on what to say, and how,
while I fumble now, my voice, like smoke rings
telescoping through each other
in this soft-lit living room. I notice only
a vase of purple irises, in my hand
a fluted paper plate with purple prints
where the spirals of pinwheel sandwiches
filled with cream cheese and sun-dried tomato paste

seem to turn, faster and faster, the Ferris wheel
at Navy Pier, its light
like pearls from a broken necklace spilling
onto the night-time mirror of Lake Michigan.

Ten Takes on Snow

1

My first winter in by Lake Michigan
covered me with white, cold, alien snow
till there was no light left
in my tropical eyes.

2

My fingers felt snow once,
long ago in Rohtang pass in the Himalayas.
Who knew one day I would be
pressed in its white pages
like a dead flower?

3

Snow's a new word I fear.
The "s" in "snow"
wraps around me like an icy tongue,
the "o" like blue lips
with the power
to swallow everything.

4

I see a girl in a far-away country
lost in a field yellow with mustard flowers.
Now, I watch a woman
staring out of the window
at a Land of Snow,
and Snow people who do not know her.

5

Numb and awkward,
my frozen fingers
grasp at snow, fresh fallen.
They try to make a snowball
like a child's first try
at kneading chappati dough.

6

Fantastical and magical
the flurries flutter and whirl,
going nowhere.
My state of mind exactly.

7

Snow-flake, snow-fall, snow-drift, snow-bound.
How do I explain snow
to friends who have never seen it?

8

My father lives on that side of the world
where winter is a moth-eaten
wool sweater worn from November to January.
Rubbing his chest while watching TV,
he watches the blizzard rage on the news.

Stay away from the snow,
he warns me on the phone.

9

When the snowstorm grew fiercer
they called it a *whiteout.*

Like you could wipe your life clean
and start again.

10

We walked knee deep in snow
like excited children.
Like fishermen
battling up a salmon-braided stream.
So much harder than
pushing through sharp-bladed rice fields

when we lived in the sun.

The Rice Fields

Miles of them grow in my carry-on
and travel with me across continents

but the customs officers are suspicious
they eye my old suitcase and ask me to open it

Pickles? they ask sniffing deeply
prodding a packet or two
say *Sure ma'am you've got no jeera or chilies?*
(now they've learned the Hindi word for cumin
so the new trick is to joke with us) And one time

I saw three burly officers question
an elderly couple disheveled
as I was from 20 plus hours of travel
and as disoriented (and yes
as usual all the usual "foreign" suspects
are sent along to "Agriculture") and
they poked around in their overstuffed bags
(where some rice fields appeared but
they couldn't see them of course) and

one officer said *Duck? Bombay Duck?*
It's a fish?? Dried fish your son
wanted? Sorry no fish allowed
or birds (The officers looked
at each other again and again:
expressions priceless) So another time I land

at Detroit airport and I shake my head
at the silver-haired officer
say *Sir, no, no pickles meat or cheese*
I buy them here at Bombay Grocers
and Patels (Give them a sweet Colgate smile)
Yes, yes, sweets, only made of lentil No dairy, no dairy

The red-gold cardboard boxes of sweets he can see
but not the rice sprouting beneath
the young green shoots

              no our rice fields he will never see
              we carry them wherever we go

What's Wrong with Wilted Lettuce

is that it isn't crisp. No one's tasted
hunger in a while, whatever's cooking
for dinner is not good enough. That's why

one day you made your daughter
watch BBC to see how flies
crowd in the eyes of dying children
on the streets of Kolkata, your city,
and now she hates you. But your neighbor

who gave you "How to Make Gingerbread
Houses" believes Girl Scouts
should have taught her
true compassion, that fortunately
the only tsunami she may ever know
is one in her bathtub, or the mild aftershocks
of boyfriend betrayal. As if you can

make her wise, be the Oracle of Delphi
you talk of war and genocide,
warn her of Ecstasy, date rape, pedophiles,
she says Mom, not pasta again.
So you tailor menus to please, know
why your mom did it, your grandma
too. Then one day she comes home

from college quoting "if the shoe doesn't fit
must we change the foot" to her father
who has settled on the couch
to watch CNN's coverage
of Syrian refugees, tells her he hopes
Assad will be history. But now you've left

the living room so it's just white
noise, and you think of voices, music,
fading in and out of the big wooden
radio when you were a girl. You turn

on your little kitchen TV while humming
snippets of "The Good Ship Lollipop"—
the LP your parents played for you
as a child, or sing a ghazal or a Hindi film
song your mother used to sing along with
on All India Radio, and your son licks salt
off his fingers as he shows you
his popcorn and penne pasta
artwork, and asks impatiently, What's

for dinner, Ma, hope it's not
chicken. You think, how shocked
you once were that food could be made
into craft as people in your old
country and war zones starved. But

now you can shrug, take the chuck
roast out of the oven, watch
survivors crossing borders
caught on video, under constant fire,
scaling razor fences, ladders
to freedom. But suddenly,

each scene
slams into your
mind, crashes into other
branded memories. Blood-
stained fabric flaps in black
and white wind, as your hands shake
as you pick quickly through lettuce,
fling wilted leaves into the bin.

Dhanya Patta

—Coliandrum; Cilantro

Tiny fringes, three-palmed leaves—

the women pulled them from fields
near the city, brought them at sunrise

to Kolkata markets
piled high in bamboo baskets,

sold them in clumps, complete
with mud and rain, thread-like

earthworms wound around the roots.
Their large-leaved pretty cousins here

are shadows I flavor my food with.
Like watered sherry in a stew,

the voice of diluted vintage is a mildness
I must appreciate. A missed beat

I listen for, a soft note's meek echo,
as if it might have been wild once,

child of woodland with the sun
leached out of its blood,

a herb afraid of itself. And garnish
you often may be, made into chutney,

marinade, masala,
stamped foreign, just a picture

in someone's cookbook, but in my kitchen
your fingers touch every dish. My tongue

wills you to taste like yourself—
rough, feisty, tickling my palate,

your green breath rises fresh,
essential as a blessing.

The Scent of an Indian

An auntie tells me
her neighbors complain
when cooking smells
float out of her window
and into their apartments.
But no one mentions the reek
of grills heating upon patios
and decks, the stench
of burning meat that wraps
around several blocks
every day.

Another shows me how
to burn incense, sandalwood
or jasmine, or beads of camphor
to clear the air of spicy smells,
and how to cleanse
the kitchen with lemon
and orange peel. Baking soda
and vinegar. And one day
a friend shares her secret—
boil a pot of coffee for awhile.
Or bake cookies, or a cake.
Let the aroma fill your hair,
your clothes, your house,
and fill the neighborhood.
Otherwise the curry smell
will follow you everywhere.
People will glare. Especially
at the office.

I get it. Ginger, garlic, cumin,
coriander, turmeric aren't
your everyday spices. But
they've been used for eons.
See how they are co-opted now?
Garam masala is a buzzword.
Turmeric capsules are a rage.

Suddenly coconut oil is a miracle.
This food is hip to some, but not
when we live, cook next door?

Yet another auntie who has lived here
a long time and now has a nice house
in the suburbs explains that she
fries fish in her garage in cold
weather. The fumes dissipate
quickly in the open air. Fresh
peppermint sprayed after.
Freed-Om.

"Free smells." You should make
a sign! Like Jimmy John's,
quips a feisty second-gen
kid when we talk about this.
Yeah, I say, and laugh. In India,
every home's cooking smells
mingle and shimmy in the streets.
Stray dogs, cats, and crows
hang around for scraps.
Sometimes a neighbor will
bring us a bowl of what
she's made. Sometimes we take
her a dish of something new,
chat over chai and Time-pass
and Good-day biscuits.

Fun facts. Vasco da Gama
sailed from Portugal, looking
for India, for spices. Opened
our world to the west. Forever.
European raiders never
stopped coming. They
conquered for cinnamon.
For pepper. Killed us
for clove, cardamom.
Tell me, whose food then
exploded with our flavors?

With the fruit of our soil, our
ancestors' blood? And when
we fry our fragrant masalas
we get complaints, curses?

Green Card

On a blazing summer day,
we are last in line,
standing at the end
of a long white vinyl shelter
swelling like a hot air balloon
full of stale perfume, restless feet,
B.O. and icy palms, just
at that very edge where
the rays of sun reach in
and grab our ankles.

Listening to many languages,
guessing what they say,
shifting from foot to foot,
we crawl closer to the door.
It is nearly two hours,
we can go inside now.

The air-conditioning cools
the beads of sweat at our temples.
We are frisked,
then line up again,
against the wall.
Children with bubble-gum
stuck to their sandals
scramble onto laps
or try to climb walls.

We sit in hard chairs
waiting for our number to be called.
Faces, tired and tense,
from every nation wait too.
Green cards dangle in the balance.
And old man with no teeth
and green sweatpants is helped inside
by a man in his twenties
wearing Harley Davidson boots.
They speak little English.
T-shirts shriek Tommy Hilfiger,

Florida, Six Flags America.
People fidget with their buttons, hair.
Those desperate to suck cigarettes
rush outside, come back quickly.

The sharp edge
of my blue passport
rips the yellow envelope,
nudges my hand.
Dust still sits
in its creases.
It remembers the old country,
knows its days
are numbered,

and like a cat in a cage,
all eyes,
lets itself be taken
to undisclosed destinations.

Walking Down a Street

in Chicago, on an summer afternoon so yellow so blue,
bright as Italian bowls at Bloomingdale's,
I look for the domestic violence shelter
where I will work next week.
The secret place where women and children
are brought at dead of night,
or in daylight as amber the alcohol

the men drink when they batter them. At the corner,
a man tips his broad-rimmed hat to me,
mouths bourbon sounds in the slant of tavern lights
says *Morning missy*, and I nod,
smile freezing as I turn into a street dull with houses,
look for a number and hope he and the two men up ahead
near the vacant lot full of green
and blue garbage bags
do not hear my quickened footsteps

or the red drum of my heart. I don't cross
the littered street but walk straight
between the slouching men who swing their arms
like puppets, sing curses like hymns,
bottles glint in brown bags in their fists.
One throws his package, and from my almost closed eyes
I see a sudden splatter of green
in the gutter, the shards embellish the pattern
of the shattered jewelry of the street—
the emeralds, the garnets, the rubies
of rage and sorrow,

and I think *they are going to kill me*—
I want to run home
just like I did in my youth on the Bright Streets,
the Dilkhushas, the Darga Roads
the New Park Streets in Calcutta
when I was happy that the drunks
who drank on the street beat each other up that night
instead of their doe-eyed wives at home
or their scarecrow children who gleaned

dinner from garbage in Tiljala and Tangra,
and I'd hold my breath, my tiny breasts shrinking
into my first Maidenform bra from Rehman's
in New Market, try not to notice the sea of red eyes
of joints, of drunks, of cigarettes swimming

like fireflies in the Guinness-thick darkness
of the entrance where in our broken mailbox
the men often stored clay pipes, foil
and matches. And I'd clamber, two steps-three
at a time, limping hard, wishing my body
were air, that it had wings to fly
up to our second floor flat, and then reaching
the dim pool of pale ale light by the door
ring the bell like a maniac

till someone opened it, my fury against my father
beating its fists on the wall, for not complaining
to the politician landlord. For not moving
us out of here. For what if the mouths
of these fiery dragons reached out of the heaving
darkness and devoured me, book bag and all
as I stumbled over mumbling bodies,
scaly feet, ragged lungis and the stench

of country liquor? *I didn't come here to die*, I think,
this flesh and blood woman with dreams,
wearing faded Levis and old *Chamba-lama*
silver earrings, to die in this back street
just like home, a road I never really left behind
but seek instead, search for more broken
shadows like my own, fall to that rank
animal whose familiar fingers
close about my throat like love
even here, in the endless, sweet daylight
of a Chicago summer.

First Walk on Avon

—*Rochester Hills, Michigan*

we walked a paved path to Kmart and Borders
where women pushed strollers trailed toddlers
joggers jogged and cyclists zoomed by ringing their bells
suddenly a car slowed down stopped by me

where women pushed strollers trailed toddlers
a window rolled down a face red and hazy
from a car that slowed down stopped by me
a mouth wide open blazed *you something fff bbb*

a window rolled down a face red and hazy
the car screeched away my jaw hung open
a mouth blazed *you mmm something fff bbb*
I nearly fell were they cursing us I stuttered

the car screeched away my jaw hung open
you didn't turn your head fixed your eyes on the path
I nearly fell were they cursing us I stuttered
don't look back you snapped don't look back

you didn't turn your head fixed your eyes on the road
keep walking move fast they may come back you said
don't look back don't look back you snapped
as we walked the paved path to Kmart and Borders

One Sunday

I saw you three darling little girls
in the parking lot of Kmart. A pink
vision of innocence

in your silky Sunday
frills, white stockings, patent leather
shoes, and you stood there holding

hands, waiting obediently while
your mother, wearing a yellow suit,
locked her green Town and Country

van. You were a trinity
of perfect cherubs all in a row.
As perfect as some of my friends'

children, or the kids of my parents'
friends who visited us from abroad,
or the dolls I played with as a child

so many years ago, and as loveable.
Your light brown hair tumbling
from bright bows

the way my own long black ringlets
once poured over my shoulders. How
I wanted to pick you up

in my arms. But I beamed love
like a lighthouse instead, reckless
and strong as the tropical sun

and suddenly, you saw me—three
pairs of honey-gold eyes met mine.
As if in a Broadway musical, and

right on cue, your soft mouths
dropped open. But there was
no sound. I was in a silent

film. Where your mother
notices me and shoots
a strange glance at me, grabs

your hands, whips you
around like little puppets, pulls
you through the doors

of the store. You disappear in a flash.
What just happened? Dizzy,
I load my bags into the trunk

of my blue Honda Civic, my own
brown eyes look back at me
in the reflection of sun-scorched

steel, the light strange but
briefly sizzling through the fog
that fills my head. Few here

look like me. Heading home,
my hands shaking
on the wheel, I tell

myself forget it, forget it—
it was only surprise
that scared them.

O Say Can You See

look into my eyes America
how easy it is
to dream in Technicolor

                        o say white say red say blue
                        and every color

we who made and make you still
we have built
your towers
your tracks your bridges
                        with our bones

from sea to shining sea this is our home
home is where the heart is
yes all the broken ones

we pick your fruit sing hosanna
we build our hearths here
                        we bake bread that we break together
we give thanks for each grain
we feed the hungry
for we have known hunger

see this mouth it sings peace
                        in every language

watch my face shine it will light up
your pavements your alleys

your castles your shacks
your thirsty fields
like a harvest moon
after blight and famine
                        and give back to us
the dollars like shekels
you have stolen forever

study then the maps inside my eyes
see the world

yes feel my heartbeat
touch my human skin
it is real

and see our scars they are the same
our scars we carry them thick and ugly
                              we are no stranger to dust and ashes
here is my war-torn hand
here are my lips let me kiss your cheek

where do we end
                              where do we begin

when I say love I mean you
when I say home I mean you

when I say to you
we are so beautiful do not turn away
                              do not shatter America America
for richer for poorer
we are your beautiful bones
your heart
your veins
are made of us
why are you afraid our blood is the same color
                              our skin so easy to dissolve
frail border between this world and the next

oh sing with me sing with me what is made one
should not be pulled asunder
we who are embraced
by sweet Lady Liberty

                              we who are made *so beautiful*
                              so varied
                              so new

so whole again
inside the harbor

of your arms oh America
we are you do you not see

do not lead us into darkness
do not
                    hate our gods our children
                    throw us not into camps prisons ghettos
                    smash your jackboots into us

but deliver yourself
from that dagger
                              the dagger you can become

2

A Funny Thing Happened

—Iargo Springs, Michigan

How many steps were there
to the bottom of the bluff?
To reach the reedy Au Sable

river? A hundred? Two?
A place we loved to visit.
Such a holy place it was once.
And on the water, the barge
is a museum where you can
see through the portholes
to where the table is laid
with plastic steaks and fried eggs
and other food the hunky
lumberjacks ate, and
you can read about the Finns,
Swedes, Germans, Italians, Danes—
all immigrants (like us) who spoke

no common language, but
created a new vocabulary
to communicate. We loved
to visit this area and told
this story to our guests—a couple
from South India. While
the men braved

the stairs, the woman and I
walked the rim. I talked about
the Native Americans who
once paddled their canoes
up the river for powwows,
camouflaged so well
when they arrived at the steep
bluff. How they would
have flourished had the white

man not landed. Think
Columbus, the Pilgrims, Clive
and the East India Company.
How for two hundred years
we Indians had struggled under
the British. I felt the weight
of history sink heavy
in my bones even as we let
the spectacular scene seep in.
Silently we watched
pygmy nuthatches dart up
and down the craggy,
ancient oaks.

Then you both
returned, panting,
exhausted. A funny thing happened,

you said, and laughed.
An old man with piercing
eyes stopped you
on your way up,
and said,
It's nice to see you.

Who was he?—you wondered.
Nice to see you too,
you'd muttered.
He wailed

I miss my darkies!

And then he burst
into tears, turned and left.
You were puzzled, you said.
You felt sorry for him, you said.

My chest heaved.
I couldn't speak.

That night, on our drive home,
as our guests slept in the back seat,
I told you what he meant.

Guests Who Came to Dinner

Guess what some of our guests said

when we told them what the man said
to my husband and his friend
the words spinning in my head
I miss my darkies

first everyone stopped eating and drinking

then one said Ha I don't know what to say
How strange muttered another
I don't know even know how I am supposed to react
and yet another said what does it all mean

and another other couple muttered softly to themselves
and looked for words and looked at their plates
and a woman who was known to be very compassionate said
Oh my with sadness
maybe he really missed old times
It's possible *right* she sighed

and her husband said people make too much of these things
and told a story about how once he and his buddies
went to a bar in Detroit and everyone stared at them all night
how intimidated they felt

and for a while everyone shook their heads this way and that

and who knows if they were bobbing a yea or nay or what
or if they thought I had made this story up
and I wondered if maybe there ever was a right time
to share such experiences

but then they kept right on eating
savoring the salmon and rice I had cooked for them
and soon they were asking me what I had made for dessert
such a good cook I was they said

Good Neighbors
(or Ham Salad or What Would Jesus Do)

It's the day after Easter.

I take out my ham salad
from the fridge.
I eat the pink
slices of salty ham and bite-
sized Red Delicious
pieces, their half-
sweet-half-
tart white flesh

that is turning
brown. I think
of my neighbor
who comments
on my brown skin

(you're so tanned,
she says
in her Southern drawl,
laughs, you don't
need to go to
the tanning studio)

and was outraged one day
when she asked me about
a crossword clue she couldn't crack
and in flash I came up with the word.
It was as if I'd stabbed her.

It was this very neighbor who sent me
these very slices of ham
(so tasty and so cold),

from her Easter feast for three—
her husband, herself, and her

"other self" or her friend— Job.
Whom she introduced to me once.
Yes, Job was there, and maybe
a few more "personalities"
lived in the apartment
below us.

Before I knew about her friends
I'd let her water my plants when
I was out of town. I found
she'd drunk our best bourbon
and filled the bottle
with muddy water—or was
it coca cola? And though
I know it's her friend Job
(and maybe more?)
who tell her what to do,
I still drive her

sometimes, to the other side
of town (to a hairdresser
she cannot afford)
because the cops
confiscated her license.

She's mixed a cocktail of pills
and booze and tried to die. And
though my heart weeps for her
I never take her to do groceries.
She may deftly
shop lift a bottle
of booze or ketchup,
an apple here or
a frozen treat there,
(or whatever her friends

want that day), and then
if she's caught, she may
flail about and scream,
sob to the security guards—

what she told me she had screamed
when the guards
at Neiman Marcus
had caught her red handed.

She said they had dragged her away
in handcuffs,
as she cried out all the while—

Please, it wasn't me! It was him, Job who did it.

"English as She Is Spoke"

1.

some common convent school rules

speak only in English
or else
we will fine you
several rupees
or break your fingers
with our canes
suspend you even
and if you answer back
(in any language)
we expel you
make your poor
vernacular speaking parents
grovel
before we take you back

remember
even the watchman we employ
has to speak in English
(and convert)
you will not get a job
even as a sweeper
imagine that they told him
the little brown boy
shivering in his skin

2.

Remember those famous English Primers
the little white boys and girls

the well-fed priests and nuns who taught you
with their wooden sticks and rulers

Hello this is Jane and this is Peter
and yes by God they will teach you English
by rote or by rod by rood
by gosh by golly they will

3.

we may have triple PhDs and win Pulitzers
even a Nobel or two

but
non-native speakers of English
they call us in America

how come you speak English they ask
how come you speak such good English

ah the British stayed for only 200 years you know
took us to the cleaners
took us to church
where they

ate our bodies drank our blood
and they sang a song of love
allelu allelu alleluia

that's why we speak
such goooooooooood English
such pure English the Queen's
English no less

4.

and when you go to school in America
(take the TOEFL exam if you apply

even if you have several degrees
and are a professor of English)

they say oh now you need to learn American English
sorry you speak Indian English and write in Colonial style

and change the rules on you again
as they put you in your place

5.

don't you know what it means when they ask
you to repeat yourself again and again
in interviews
or when you meet someone and they say
oh you have an accent
where are you from
no where are you really from
(ah you have an accent they say
so charming)

and
when your students challenge you
to explain your comments on their essays
(yes try to bully you)
to change their grades
saying

no it's you
you don't understand what we mean

6.

some of the great learned ones
in academia
may say to a student your English
is *Colonial* and say oh it's your second
language. ESL! That label will stick
forever! And sometimes they might
even give you lower grade

and when you teach
folks may tell you
how brilliantly you taught that class
(so surprised) tell you you're smarter
than you look (with a look of genuine
admiration)

and sometimes even a very bright person,
will exclaim
see you how lucky you are
that your country was colonized
just as well just as well don't you think
they will say and then beam at you

don't you see (wide smile)
just imagine (imagine!)
now you are teaching
in our schools and colleges

The Suburban Car Dealership Shuttle Driver

Hell I have no idea where she wants to go

says the shuttle driver as he glares at me
with his hard gray eyes and as I tell him where I want to go
he says Huh What What's that you say

Face unsmiling old arms sagging he turns completely
in the seat to look me in the eye asks again what's that you say
I repeat *I live near Trader Joe's* his face burns red
says I don't get it don't get it

The new Trader Joe's store I say slowly
the one opposite Oakland University you know

He could be a little younger than my father
I know he doesn't think he's hard of hearing
raising his voice he tells me he can't understand immigrants

I say our accents are different can be confusing
tell him I'm an English teacher have been for 16 years
No kidding he says looks at me hard
swerves to miss a car

Don't they know they should speak English
if they want to live here
My father came from all the way from Russia
he knew English and even Polish he did he did

but me I don't know Russian
I'm not one for languages and that kind of stuff
And you he asks Four languages I say was brought up bilingual
Huh no kidding he says
his driving's jerky

foot heavy on the brake stares at me hard
forgets where to turn to pick up the woman waiting
near *Nino Salvaggios's* Tells me twice

she needs to be dropped off first though he picked me up
first Ah how he has to keep everyone happy

Now why do they all come here
Yeah yeah high salaries
I know I know
What if you want a new life I say
for you for your kids Yeah hmmm he says chews his cheek
asks do you have family in your country
Yes, parents in their eighties friends students yes

He runs a red light looks puzzled asks do you see them often
Once in two years maybe too expensive I miss them

He's missed *Nino's* long ago he brakes hard frowns
clucks Hell did you see it he asks we passed it I say
Hell you should've told me swings the old van around

mid-turn says I retired from Ford Financial
they fired contractors couldn't understand them
wouldn't speak English and the other day huh

had this old man to drop off an oriental he was from Chrysler
Hell I had no idea where he wanted to go
They should all learn English

They do I say they do
some are better at it than others
they struggle hard all day
all day like my students at Oakland Community College
working shifts working three jobs working at grammar
late into the night so they can go to college rush to class eyes red
become doctors lawyers engineers

Yeah he says
yeah like that cancer doctor I took my wife to see
Had to drop him he was a...can't remember what they call
cancer doctors huh had a long name too and boy
we couldn't get a word he said
Had to let him go sucks a quick breath
Does your husband speak English

I say fluently No kidding he says

Where my husband works I say there are folks from all over the world
speaking English with different accents and many
don't understand each other but it's OK

No kidding he says and bellows loudly whacks my hand pushes back
his Redwings cap with both hands
The van wanders Cars honk all around I wince
It is fifty minutes
since I stepped into this van It is only fifteen from the dealership
on Rochester Road to my apartment Here we are he says
squints as I open the door says You're an interesting woman

I try to smile I am so drained We learn
yes we learn from each other I say
I hand him a newsletter from the community college
point to a story written by my student from Sierra Leone
whose arm was cut off when she was a little girl
and who lives with her American parents
He frowns at the paper and at me
his lips are taut

Have a nice day I say thank you

What's that you say he asks gray eyes harder than before
face unsmiling arms sagging
he turns completely in the seat asks again What
What's that
you say

Yet Another Welcome

we went to Bangkok Cuisine
in the heart of downtown
near DQ where teenagers
gather like bees
it was close to closing time
and we ordered crispy fried duck
and pork pot stickers
relaxing into the seats we looked out

of their big glass picture
window and the neon sign
with missing letters
blinked and blinded us
so it took us a few extra
minutes to see the puckered
faces clustered there
mouthing words
fingers flipping the bird

then running
then turning around again
ready to flash us the pale
moons of his butt

their laugher echoing
for decades

25 Responses
(or Pick-a-Combo or Take It as You Like It)

1. This happened here? But it's such a welcoming place.
2. What? I'm sure you misunderstood.
3. They'll get used to seeing you. This happens everywhere.
4. Ignore them! It's ignorance, nothing else.
5. Ah, they're jealous to see immigrants doing well.
6. You should see the way some people treat me at the office.
7. Here? Really? Are you sure? Hmmm.
8. Oh my. I'm so sorry.
9. Crickets.
10. They get up and walk away.
11. They shift in their chairs and change the subject.
12. You're not the only ones who suffer.
13. Please come to our church next Sunday? We welcome everyone.
14. At least they didn't have guns.
15. Who told you to leave our home and go so far away?
16. Do you know that Black folks are shot everyday?
17. Didn't you know before you came how racist this country is?
18. There's so much discrimination in India, why make such a fuss?
19. How do people treat Muslims in India? And what about caste?
20. Things are worse now all over the world. We thought we'd come a long way.
21. What's new? Segregation, segregation, segregation!
22. Have you heard of reverse racism?
23. Will you go back to India?
24. When will you go back to India?
25. When will you come home?

Someone Rings and Rings the Bell

I shut my ears I do not respond to the call

I am writing a poem
about Shiva and Parvati

and the universe is spinning
burning up in his tandava
his final no-holds barred
destruction dance

then whoever it is at my apartment door
in Auburn Hills stops ringing
and knocks and knocks and knocks
and won't go away darn
it must be the ones who leave
flyers showing hell with spectacular
fires and people screaming and
heaven with blue skies and woolly clouds

by now Parvati has awakened
and will soon begin her dance of words
on my page
and there is a chance a real chance
of peace
of divine union

but they still knock

finally I go and ask politely who is it
a sweet voice replies
Melissa Melissa she says
we have come to hand you
an invitation

I open the door
to two lovely young women
one brown haired and primly
skirted and bloused as if visiting her ancestors
in her office clothes and the other one

a smiling blonde and a petite companion
with a look that says
no we are not here to sell you anything
we are friendly people
come come to our church her eyes say

look no one is allowed to solicit here I'm about to say
but I say hi and grin and the blonde one
gives me a flyer see we want to invite you
her manicured hands hold a leather folder
thank thank you I say hurriedly almost
snatching it from her hands
have a nice day they chime
wave their hands

but Shiva's is not ready for delays
and fake thank yous

his arms are raised up above my head
ready to shatter me smash me
with his fiery feet
set my city on fire
with his third eye
what will happen next what will happen

I hurry back to my desk
call out to Parvati who will dance

and save us all
Oh please let

let the Ganga flow and appease his anger
let the clouds burst over us
quench the world's thirst

but I am curious to see what's in the colorful
flyer so I take a peek
at the invitation the women gave me

Oh really it's a barbeque party
that I've been invited to

on the expensive card
is a procession of happy people
and they all seem to be rushing somewhere

well-dressed kindly folk
with their children and some elderly folks trailing
and one or two couples who are black
are skipping along too
I don't see any brown-skinned ones
maybe we are welcome too who knows
they want to add us to the flock

but the sky in the background of the picture
is heavily streaked with clouds
and the dark sky is being torn apart by lightning
still the folks in the pretty picture look as calm
as my well-heeled visitors who came to my door
and march on in their bright clothes
march determinedly to the edge
of the margin of the card

enough enough

I say to myself
I've ignored Shiva too long
left him waiting

too long his mad wild hair flowing
behind him as the world turns turn turns
but now the words on the invitation catch my eyes

How you can survive the end of the world

and then in small print below—
you are warmly invited
to come and listen to the answer

ah the destruction of the world cannot be halted now
I fling the "Keep on the watch" threat card on the floor
turn to my page to start up the tandava again

no escape
I will surely
be struck
by lighting

by the God of Abraham and my ancestors
by the God of the happy people with bright clothes
or by the fiery trident of blue-skinned Shiva

Herstory

She was born in Mumbai, right? Marathi is her mother tongue.

Her mother's father worked in the Port Trust in Karachi. It was not Pakistan then. Her father was a marine engineer who sailed around the world.

Joseph? There are names like that in India? There are *Jews* in India?

South Asian Diaspora. First generation. Immigration. Assimilation. Acculturation.

Music? Judaic and Christian hymns, Hindi film songs, pop, rock, blues and jazz. And ein kliene classical music. Western and Eastern.

At 6, she got polio. No one knew what it was at first. No one knew if she would ever walk again.

Her great grandfather was the magistrate of the state of Aundh in Maharashtra. Her grandfather was a doctor who served in Egypt during World War I. They said he died from "shell shock".

What? All this time I thought you were Hindi. Oh sorry, Hindu.

Bene Israel. Also known as Indian Jews. Said to be shipwrecked on the Konkan coast first century BC. Some say seven men and seven women survived.

From an "English-speaking home." Catholic Convent educated. Has several degrees. Does not want to marry.

OMG. How do know so much about animal, birds, Nature? Did you learn all this after you came to the US?

Became a high school English teacher in an Anglican Boys' School. Mother Teresa lived in Mother House across the road from this school. For Children's day Mother Teresa was invited. The senior boys and teachers sang in the choir.

Widowed at 33, her grandma. Sold her jewelry to support three small sons.

She and her husband struggled. Lived with her parents, took care of them as they grew old. Then she and her husband left and went far, far away to make a new life.

Jeopardy is her jam. Was among the top quizzers in India. Once upon a time.

Her grandmother spoke, read and wrote *sudh* Marathi. Hebrew prayers in prayers books were written in Marathi. *Eliahu ha'navi. Elaihu ha'navi.*

Post-colonialism. Transculturalism. Multiculturalism. Cosmopolitanism. Ism.

Nolen gurer sandesh. If friends from Kolkata visit, they bring her those sweets. From Mithai. In Park Circus. Where she used to live.

So what about your first name? That's not Indian at all!

On the old ship Dufferin a bad-tempered Scotsman whipped her dad regularly, denied him shore leave. He never saw his mother for weeks at a time.

Dreams in English. Quarrels with English.

Every day the cadets on the training ship had to sing "Rule Britannia". The food was horrible. My dad and his friends sang "The cutlets in the NCC they say are mighty fine, one rolled off the table and killed a friend of mine".

Not religious. Respects all religions. A free spirit. A bit woo woo.

One day someone told her about something called Post Polio Syndrome. It felled Joni Mitchell. A relapse that paralyzes overworked strong muscles.

Trafalgar Square with pigeons. With Galapagos tortoises. With the Schwartings in Germany. Her parents' many voyages. Lost photographs.

Before she left for the US, her students gave her flowers and gifts. Will you have a gun there, one asked? Another said, hah, this is what they call the brain drain. Still another said ma'am you have betrayed us. She will always remember their eyes. Many still write to her today.

Since her mother died, she hasn't returned to Kolkata.

God of the Great Blue Window

—For Trayvon Martin, Breonna Taylor, George Floyd, and for all people of
color who have been brutally slain

What tide washed me out of this sea

swept me to another shore O God of the great
blue church window that looks like the ocean
from the outside O say can you see

whose shore whose sea is this
for they do not know me here

outside of the water culture
where fish flourish and grow

whose fish I ask whose culture
how fast how slow shall I swim and in whose ocean

will you see through my skin
my covered head
I who swam my blue path home while
the night sky spun in the blue blue rain

fish out of water

fish in a storm in the big blue window
whose fish whose water whose storm I ask
whose world
filled with the sound of distant waters
in the flood of no-mercy tides
whose child lifted on whose shoulder
whose child whose mother left behind

fish live on land

whose fish I ask whose land I ask
whose boat whose watch whose feast whose hunger

which fisherman lifting his silver net in the night
which angel
counting the blue blue shadows
singing and pointing

yes you yes you yes you yes you
my name itself a prayer yes
my name itself a wish
my name itself the crashing surf
my name itself turning on itself

on land I breathe uneasy

O blue window churning with a million blind eyes
the wave roaring
but everything silent on the inside
how quickly I swam through the bluest eye

clean as a fish
my fins beating slow
                    then fast fast fast

or was it fast then
                    slow slow slow

    —after Lorna Goodison's "God a Me"

3

Hunting White Tigers in Kipling Country

—Madhya Pradesh, India

To the Indian kings—the royal shikaris,
hunting came as naturally as ownership of kingdom,

and the killing of tigers, especially a hundred and one
white tigers in one lifetime (may the gods preserve

and keep the kingly race, the blood
of tigers give long life and many sons)

was considered auspicious. From father to son,
son to father the game rooms grew

through the length of palaces (modeled on Versailles)
filling with striped and spotted pelts, horned trophies, and sometimes

one single black and white photograph of a grand old hunt
stretched from wall to palace wall. Soon the rajas

invited white sahibs on shikar too, hoping
manly camaraderie with the ruling race

(Long live! And cheers to the gin and tonic, the soft
tones of sunlight on the enormous verandahs,

the reshmi-kababs served by turbaned servants)
would buy them time, help spare

their hunting grounds. With fanfare and guns
they would set out, but only after thousands of villagers

sent out at dawn beat drums, combed bristling jungles
till tigers leapt from cover

and dashed madly toward the wall of elephants
from whose backs the bejeweled rajahs

and sola-topeed sahibs thundered a monsoon of bullets—
felling every creature that fled

toward them. Perhaps some birds escaped
through the storm of dust, blood

and death-roars. But to ensure continuance of blessing
and bounty at the hands of mighty gods

and the mightier British,
(O how the sun never set

in those kingdoms) the hunt went on till
101 white tigers, maybe a few less Bengals,

leopards, sloth bear, wild dog and cat, deer, hare,
boar, antelope and bison were dragged

by loyal subjects (who can name these
humble natives, their children's children,

their mortal terrors?) who laid them side by side
in a never-ending road (and what was the length

of those sepia-tinted hunt room
photographs?) from sunrise to sunset. Turn

your head from the wall on the east
to the wall on the west. Inhale the mothball

and brimstone smell. Witness the blood-
blasted fur. Count each black and white

stripe, count every color, count as they mark
the mud with their sprawled

bodies, (drawn claws now sheathed), become
one long red carpet in the dust.

A-Z of Foreign Anguish

A is for anguish says my mummy tongue, my lingo lango la la
But English is my foreign father tongue daddy lang blab blab
Colonists with your white gaze told our stories. With classic
demagoguery, tyranny, manifest destiny, excuses, you forged
evil tales to transform us into demons. Crushed truths with vile,
flippant lies. What about us? How you ravaged us? Scepter and staff
grind down our culture. Kings of erosion and erasure, how long
has your terror ruled? Your knives at our children's throats? Who wash
Indians out of every picture? Who conquered our lands crying—I
just come in peace! Guns in your hearts, greed in your DNA. The Raj
kept us slaves in our own land! Took our tea, spices, jewels, broke our back,
lashed and tortured us. What's in your Crown? Our Kohinoor! Oh cruel
masters! Recorders of the "inferior race". Ah, clever sahib and mem!
Natives? Like insects you labeled us! With fine calipers, condescension.
Oppressor, the nightmare still lives, the hate systems that never go.
Pain is embedded in our bones. You poisoned our wells. Now, you dump
questions on us? You teach us civility? Listen to our Q&A, our A&Q
right out of our mouths. You shoved the father tongue down our
"savage" (and shithole countries') throats. Destroyed histories, literatures,
tongues. Made us ugly in our own eyes, made us hate ourselves, split
us, shattered us, turned Hindu against Muslim, Muslim against Hindu.
Viceroys and priests, you ruled, you hunger-converted us. Oh holy Rev.
Whiteman, was sweet Jesus' face fair? He was a humble dark-skinned Jew!
Xanax—will it help? When we invite you to our open table, you vex
yourself! You cry we're your current foreign anguish? That we can sway
zeitgeist, world biz, karma. Got heart? Got Hinglish? Chutzpah? Pizzazz?

—after "Discourse on the Logic of Language" by M. NourbeSe Philip

The Night Babri Mosque Falls

—Kolkata, December 6, 1992

It is Saturday. My husband and I eat hot and sour soup—green with chilies, coriander, and try the new house special—Calcutta hakka chow at Embassy Chinese Restaurant on Chowringhee. Saul, the restaurant owner, sits down to have a drink with us, talks about how bad business is at his hotel in Darjeeling. Gorkhaland rebels are raiding everyone, there is violence everywhere.

We ask if Josh, his son, is safe. *Yes, yes, for now* he says.

I tell Saul he looks good—as tough as Tenzing. He pats his Buddha-belly and says he could never summit Mt. Everest. Tonight, we are his only customers. Strange for a Saturday. It should be loud today—like on Temple Street, Tangra, old Chinatown. He goes to fetch more wontons.

He returns with a face suddenly aged, deeply grooved.

Jaw tight, he tells us the Hindu Kar Sevaks—the saffron-clad zealots, just attacked Babri Masjid. As they scale the three ancient domes, they shatter brick after brick of the house of Allah; their pick axes and hammers reclaim the Hindu shrine inside—the one that was there *first*, the Sevaks say, before Babar conquered India and built the masjid over the birthplace of their Lord Rama.

Scholars say *False.*

They argue they argue. But we are afraid that Ayodhya—the Nazareth of the Hindus will be cinders before morning. *Ayodhya means the land of no war*, I say softly. *How could this happen after Independence?* Finishing our conversation quickly, we step out of the heavy wooden doors carved with dragons into one of the busiest streets in this city of ten million.

Ayodhya means the land of no war, I say to myself.

Outside, not a beggar, not a drunk, nor dog around. It is so empty that our footsteps echo, we can hear the neon signs on the Exide Building buzz. Our motorbike starts like a bomb going off and we speed home through the completely deserted streets, shivering inside our leather jackets. The silence of this deafening city crashes on our helmets as we ride faster and faster, our breath rapid as bullets, the noise of the Enfield's engine follows like a line of explosions.

Park Circus is a ghost town.

Everything is shut down, sealed. Silent. Holding hands wet with sweat, we run to the unguarded entrance and up the stairs. Ring the bell. My father's good eye appears at the peep hole.

The night-time bolts grate.

His voice is low. *Come in quick* he says, grey eyebrows bristle as he shuts the door softly but I know he wants to slam it. *Where were you, you idiots?* His teeth grind. *Do you know what they can do to you?*

They want blood again. Like Partition. We've lived through this once. The bastards, they want riots between Muslims and Hindus. There are already fires in Tiljala.

Check the windows he tells my husband, then together they lift the wooden bar, secure the door.

Stones strike the pavement. We hear footsteps. Running, running, running. Screams break out on the street.

Fools! Will they ever learn, he growls, and commands me *Switch off that light. Go tell your Mum you're home.*

Mama, Who'd Have Thought

that after all these years in America, my love and I
would finally have a place of our own? No, not a real
house house but a condo beside a pond. Not a real
pukur like the lakes in Bengal that dad used to go
fishing in but a man-made pond with a fountain where

Mallards and black ducks bring their broods
of super-charged little ones. And where
the pied grebe pops up in spring and fall,
and the trumpeter swans I love so much visit too.
Then the old regulars—a belted kingfisher and
a couple of blue herons fish here. Sometimes

in deep summer, cormorants unfurl and sun
their long wings to dry while still skimming
the water. Dad would love this. Now you've
come to see me, ma, let's go for a walk.
Here, take my arm and let me guide you

down slowly to the bank. The pavements
are smooth—not like those death traps
in Kolkata. You're laughing. But careful, here
the ground is uneven and slopes sharply

to the pond. You're right, that clump of grass
is where the geese I told you about nested
last year. The very same year we moved
in. So sad. Oh, the neighbors are friendly,
no, no one here is like us. Wait, let me show

you the giant goldfish. How the big ones wriggle
as the heron tries to swallow them. If
it rains tonight we'll surely see some shoals
churning on the surface. And so funny, once
when the kingfisher caught a fish that was too

heavy, or maybe it was thrashing too hard, she
must have dropped it. For days we wondered

who left this dead goldfish on our patio. A sign
from the spirit world that you live in now,

we thought! And then, you won't believe this—
one afternoon we see an osprey!
It hovered and plunged
into the pond, emerged with a goldfish
the size of a kitten in its talons and it flashes
right past the big picture window, not two feet
from where my love and I watched, mouths
hanging open. Yes, we took a photo but it was all so
sudden. It's all blurry. I'll show you when

we go back in. It happened so fast. That gorgeous
bird stayed for two weeks. I think it will return
this fall. The red-tailed hawks
and Cooper's hawks are always hunting
around here. What? Are we safe?

Yes. Yes. And no.
No, Ma, America is not safe. Sure, some policemen
kill people who don't look like them—it's scary.
White men march nowadays, shouting threats.
They put children in cages at the border. Have

they no hearts? Bad things could happen
to us here too. This is our home now, Ma.
You didn't want us to leave. You wept
for days. Forgive us. We could not bring
you here then. Now your spirit is here.
Protect us. Please stay.

Food Trouble

John Lewis, I have to ask you about this.
Some of our people cook on their decks
in summer, and in garages in fall and winter.
Now, it's the first time I ever
owned a home of my own.
And one gloomy fall afternoon
I cooked a pork butt in my slow
cooker in my garage. A neighbor
ran to my door whining
that her house was filled
with smells. But how could
that be? Firewalls can be
porous? A month later, I cooked
again, used fans, air fresheners.
This time she ambushed me
in my garage. Have I no right

to cook what I want and
where I want in my house?
Tell me, John Lewis! I need
your help. And now she wants
to bring some "specialist"
to examine my garage.
No way I'll allow this

snooping around. Will she
cause trouble, John Lewis?
Isn't this all my business?
She's odd. But what the heck,
so am I. But then—I forget,
I'm brown.

OK, so here's what
happened next. One day
the condo-association-prez
(who's quite helpful) asks me
advice about gardening, or
something about plants. We go

outside, we look. Talks sweet.
Damn! It was a cheap ruse
to tell me my neighbor
had "spoken to her". Did not
see that coming, John Lewis!

It could've been the wind?
Ha ha! she says. Then she leans in,
grinning, asks, what were you
cooking? Something spicy? Ha ha!
OMG. Did I hear right?
What? I mumbled out, in shock.
Hadn't I told that lady we would
talk? Why tell the prez?
Such a pleasure to talk
to you, my dear. Ugh!
My skin crawls even now.
Are you happy here?—she asks.
I mumble something about trees,
no privacy. I'm shaking.

When my breathing settled,
I called her out politely
in a formal email. No! She
really wanted my opnion
on planting butterfly bushes.
So sorry she "brought it up".
Right. I must have "stupid"
stamped on my forehead.

I lie awake at night. Stare
at the ceiling. Is this a nice way
to say we need to go? Is it
ignorance? Some kind of
intimidation? Brush it off
like you did with the rude
maintenance manager.
You're over-reacting?
That's what they always

say, right? When we call
a spade
a spade?

They're good folks, John
Lewis. I've got a few friends
here. I'm not very social.
I chat with them, smile. But
now in my prayers, I'm chanting—
OMG. OMG. Don't sweat it,
I know my love will say
to me. Don't
rock the boat.
But my dear,
the boat
is being rocked.
The water
is being
troubled.
Over my food
there's
a storm
brewing.

John Lewis, friend of the people,
come sit in my open garage,
I'll set a table. We'll drink
cold beer. Break bread,
talk about what's going on.
And our akka, Kamala.
When the food police
come sniffing, we'll raise
our glasses, and just
keep on cooking.

Live to Eat

All I think about is food.
The TV programs I watch
are all about food, food, food. Alton
Brown dressed as Colonel Sanders,
talking Southern, making crispy fried
chicken, his food anthropologist
Deb adding her kernels of info,
the food police arriving in helicopters
to confiscate his raw egg egg-nog.
Beat Bobby Flay—where Bobby
flays his opponents. How much
I learned from *Confucius was a Foodie*,
Lucky Chow, The Chew. I know
enough (or think I do) to write a book
full of cooking tips and my origin stories.
My eyes are fixed on those jewel-cut
vegetables, the hand-pulled noodles, the
hands of the maker of pigeon pie, foraged
truffles, chianti swirling and breathing,
the bottles of single malt being turned daily
in cellars in Scotland and Ireland.

While Covid strikes the world, and death
waits to knock on our door, I crave
a cocktail. While lungs brim with
coronavirus and bodies pile up
in morgues, in streets, I switch
between news and food channels.
I cheer on Maneet Chauhan. YES!
She won *Tournament of Champions*!

Some world leaders move fast to quell
the plague. Some, like the saffron-robed
king of India condemn the poorest
to death-marches and starvation,
and the police beat those who leave
their homes during curfew.
Lockdown after lockdown.

Skinny and sickly as a child I played
with my food, threw bread I did not
want to eat to our dog under the table.
Once, an Auntie told me she never
wasted a crumb. Told me about how
Churchill's laws caused the great
Bengal famine—how in Calcutta starving
people who looked like skeletons lay
strewn on pavements, and one day
a man walking by puked on the street
and several men who could still walk
ran up and scooped up his vomit and ate it.
Who would not be haunted by that forever?

How can I forget the beggars, the crippled
children tugging at my school-girl
sleeves, the bedraggled women
with hungry infants on their hips.
We gave alms, we gave food. But how to
feed millions? My mother stocked
cupboards and the refrigerator well.
Even during bandhs, riots, emergencies
we never went hungry. God bless
my hard-working parents,
the sacrifices they made.
May they rest in peace.
So glad they do not have to suffer
what the world is suffering now.

The crowned virus has struck every land.
The Angel of Death does not pass over.
He lingers at doorposts. His magnificent
robes touch palaces and slums.
My doors are shut. I hardly
go out. I fill my freezer with
more and more take-out. When Covid
closed down everything, I watched
long lines of cars at food banks
in the US, and in India, hungry
people being given food and water
by ordinary citizens who could

barely feed themselves. But the
government and the great Kahuna
was AWOL. My phone was flooded
with videos of migrant workers
walking hundreds of miles towards
home. No transport, no food, no water.
Jobless, homeless, overnight.

Then the cyclone hit Kolkata.
Hurricanes, floods there, and wildfires
here. Is there no end to suffering?
And in the most prosperous and powerful
country on earth thousands still die
everyday, and the orange-faced leader
shrugs. His yellow-bellied minions
laugh. Criminal negligence?
Let people of color die? Is this a kind
of genocide? This is how they care
for us? And now the mutated virus rages
on in India. No hospital beds open, no
oxygen, no firewood to cremate, no
room to bury loved ones. Still the
leaders do not cancel Kumbh Mela
and the virus spreads like blessings.
And since it is election time, the mighty
PM orders all to go vote.
Yes. While they take their last breaths?
Will democracy survive in India
and America? God help us all.

Death rules the planet. Hunger
is everywhere. Still, I am safe.
For now. For those like me, whom
luck has favored, our bellies are
never empty. We send our small
donations to charities everywhere.
Gleaners, World Central Kitchen
(Go Chef Jose Andres!), Vibha
(Go Chef Vikas Khanna!), Calcutta
Rescue (Go my friends!), and Covid
relief organizations. Pray for our

homeless, jobless, bereaved,
and dying brothers and sisters. Just
tiny drops, just tiny drops
of good intention in this vast
ocean of human pain.

And so, I trick my human brain.
The one that lives to eat, while
others eat to live—or go without.
Freeze guilt with every bite,
numb memory, send checks,
check on friends and family
via Whatsapp. Weep for those
I've lost, calm my nerves with
cooking shows, share a bowl
of chips and a vodka or two with
my love, load up my shelves, my
freezers with food. Bless the hands
of every farmer, laborer, picker,
packer, transporter, that touched
each bag or box of food! Oh all who
work at Trader Joe's, Bombay
Grocers, Meijer's, Kroger's,
Costco, Patel's! You rock.
You are our rock. You feed
us all. You feed,
you save my soul.

4

Freedom Song with Ginsberg, Dylan, Marley

It occurs to me that I am America

> Ginsberg can you rant to us
> Dylan can you moan to us
> Marley can you wail to us

American you are beautiful
sometimes you have the biggest heart I know
sometimes you have the smallest heart I know
but please
get out of the way if you can't lend a hand
for the times they are a changin'

O prophets of the people
will the walls keep marching on

are we
disposable animals

Come you masters of war you that build all the guns
it's your own children you riddle with bullets
fling upon the rubbish heap of history

I say nothing about my prisons nor the millions of underprivileged who live in my
flowerpots under the light of five hundred suns

the giants of the castle have no mercy
they grind our bones to make their bread
eat our little children fee fi fo fum

O prophets and militias of Mammon
and Machiavelli and Monsanto
Even Jesus would never forgive what you do

> O let us sing our true true songs
> our songs of freedom

Emancipate yourselves from mental slavery
oh emancipate yourself
emancipate yourself

None but ourselves can free our minds

Whose Voices Were Heard

*—A collage drawn from world and colonial history, myth, literature, scriptures,
folk and fairy tales, musicals, popular and religious songs, stories re-imagined*

O King of Experimenters
        we are put in cages by you
        in internment camps
        in laboratories

        stone walls do not a prison make
        nor iron bars a cage
                but then you the genius
                find solutions
                to every problem

                how cold your fingers
                how sharp the needles
                how fast the bullets
                how powerful the gas

~

three blind mice three blind mice
see how they run
see how they run

O the faces of indigenous races extinguished
the blurry sepia photographs
the piles of bodies
the persecuted who flee
every day carrying
their children on their backs
                who chooses who must be or not be
                and who must be flayed shocked burned
                baked impaled crucified

ever sharp the carving knife the carving knife

~

give us give us
give us this day our daily opiates
give us
our bright path to the dream
morphine an undeserved treat
chloroform a rare gift
painless bliss
how can this be wrong

we are your tired your poor your maimed your downtrodden

~

go then
                    market your heroin and cocaine
                    your love potions and snake oils
                    feed your happy pills to the masses
                    for in this laboratory of great causes and
eternal experiment
                    it is always bright
                    your million mercenaries write the laws
                    you become the law
how can this be wrong

~

        hell how can this be wrong

as if the box cars passing through villages were filled with lowing cattle
as if no one saw and heard and there was never any graffiti
as if anyone cared about crossings
what ships carried inside them
who wrote the code
who begat begat and begat the seamless legacy
who cracked it hacked it reenacted it

as if no one saw the murdered heads arranged all in a pretty row
in the panting refrigerators in the panting heat in the heart of darkness

ah the stories
by whom and for whom and of whom
justified by what book
what blue-eyed beauty
what bull or bear-
headed god

ah the stories never told
and the stories told and told but never heard

~

OK Relax of course there is escape   there are dreams
watch TV & travel channel   surf for catalogues of sand
and sea or mountain   and prairie come on big boy get your welcome drink
John Wayne my man of true grit   see the lovely natives dance   watch
the girls are young and tender the men are brave make them dance catch them
in your corrals it is high noon now dear Indiana Jones jump and jive
and jump and jive   save them from themselves
Oh the poor pagans just like in the movies

powwow powwow   this land is our land   we can kill all your bison
abduct all your little ones and in one fell swoop baptize and rape
and sodomize them Bless our brave hearts

yeehaw yeehaw you've even designed the fabulous set the clothes
the colors the spaghetti western of westerns created the new culture
written the Oscar-winning script the primer to color and colony
my how your movies can make genocide look good

~

who mentor
who tormentor
who knows when it is true morning or night
above searchlights gleam like stars
promising salvation
the bells ring we leap up
what's the buzz
tell me what's a-happening

what's the buzz
Pilate washes his soft hands
somewhere water turns to wine

~

great saint of nonviolence
Ben Kingsley played you well
whose story did they tell whose story did they kill

dear fakir my good fellow from South Africa
our high caste lawyer of nonviolence
who fought the good fight

did you really break our chains
can you stop them from garlanding
the Dalit leader's statue with shoes

stop them from breaking into Muslim homes
to kill them for the lie of hiding banned beef
true or false true or false

O prime minister yes prime minister
Of liberation we sing, O fathers of independence
how tainted is our blood

when caste lives forever
in the minds of our children
will they ever break these chains

~

who created the museums of race
in Europe's towns in Europe's towns

your race museums your
lavish kunstkammers and wunderkammers
believe-it-or-not worlds

freak shows and science circuses
record newly-bought or conquered bodies
you even invented a "grid" to measure our features

to list the lift or droop
of breast or penis
calculate how soon a baby can be taken
how much a mother will cry
and for how long

for look O look
pity him

O look the white man's burden is heavy
look how heavy it is

~

Let us examine the evidence
the gaze
the artifacts the skin and teeth of the stolen horse
the dry-bone remains of lost tribes

blue is the blood of the almighty

O bring the good news to the new worlds
Awake Arise
let us save you poor savage
from yourself

for it is decreed

we shall go forth and find great lands "dark" continents
bind them in holds of ships and feed them salt pork
and we shall forever drink mint juleps
as we shall adorn the trees with strange fruit
as we teach them to gather cottony salvation
they will be done so done so done

what saccharine unction will your tongue taste
who will give your parched mouth water

who is this maker who unmakes us
        mote by mote
        smite by smite
        and smote by smote

~

Mother, mother. mother
there's too many of you crying
        will you say why have you forsaken me
        will you say forgive them for they know not what they do
        will you shoot will you put your hands up and still be shot
        will your neck be knelt upon till your breath is gone
        will you say this is all illusion maya O maya
        will you say I am not my body
        will you say what's going on
Brother, brother, brother
will there be a time for us a place for us

~

with our shattered faces we have roamed the wilderness

        we have a dream
        so let us never
        forget our roots our passage

Michael row your boat ashore
I'm only going over Jordan
I can swim till I drown
way down upon the Sewanee River
and if Noah won't have us
let us wade in the water
O even in Hades salvation is not free
keep a coin for Charon
a crumb for Cerberus

we have a dream
and we have the music
sing *Bandhe Mahataram Bandhe Mahataram*
we're gonna trouble the water

~

where the mind is without fear and the head is held high
O my people I shall go

let my people go
        we die soon we die too soon
        we who only stand and wait

     go then to Lourdes to Luxor to Lethe
     to Delphi to Hardwar to Lumbini
     to Assisi to Brindavan to Sedona
     whatever floats your boat

this is your ancestor's ark
rise rise up singing

~

still I rise still I rise
O sing in our own myriad tongues
     in our own voices
     m'pnei tikkun ha-olam

the goddess dances on the head of the demon
the Madonna crushes the snake with her foot
Tamaso ma jyotir gamaya
from darkness unto light

do you know how to make a peaceful road
through human memory

     we know where we're going
     yes we know where we're from

may we move freely
through the passage between lives

can you see us dancing in the dark and in the rain
and in the moonlight the firelight the lamplight

dancing in the sun
in our own shining skin
in our beautiful bones

5

Prayer

O dearly beloved   you walked upon
this beautiful earth   we honor your footprints
your life   your last breath

we who never knew you we always knew you
we will cover your body with flowers as we say
your name your holy name

we will light
the match to light/the branch that will set your funeral pyre/on fire/who
will shave their heads/in mourning/light a diya/and sail a leaf boat
on the River Ganga/*Om shantih*

carry
you to the great Tower of Silence/on our shoulders/to the graveyard
of the Worshipers of Fire/offer your body to the sacred
birds/give your body back to nature

we will say Hail Mary
full of grace for you/ashes to ashes/dust to dust/a soul
has risen/let perpetual light shine upon you

we will dig
a grave for you/bow to the east/say Janazah for you/O elevate
your station among those who are guided

close
your eyelids/with loving fingers/sing Kaddish/pray grant us peace and a happy
life/light candles/to remember you

call on the Compassionate ones
ask for your heart/our hearts/to be opened/that loving kindness/guide us
to see/beyond blindness

one day
may the bullets knives nooses knees hands of hate war tyranny
burst into roses

may all darkness that lives among us inside us around us
bloom into jasmine

may pain be transformed into lilies
sweet scent lifting us all to new light

About the Author

Zilka Joseph was born in Mumbai, and lived in Kolkata. Her work is influenced by Indian/Eastern and Western cultures, and her Bene Israel roots. She has been nominated several times for a Pushcart, for a PEN America Award, Best of the Net, has won many honors, and participated in literary festivals and readings. She has been featured on NPR/Michigan Radio, and in several international online interviews and journals. Her work has appeared in *Poetry, Poetry Daily, The Writers' Chronicle, Frontier Poetry, Kenyon Review Online, Michigan Quarterly Review, Beltway Poetry Review, Asia Literary Review, Poetry at Sangam, The Punch Magazine, Review Americana, Gastronomica,* and in anthologies such as *101 Jewish Poems for the Third Millennium, The Kali Project, RESPECT: An Anthology of Detroit Music Poetry, Matwaala Anthology of Poets from South Asia* (which she co-edited*), Cheers To Muses: Contemporary Works by Asian American Women, Uncommon Core: Contemporary Poems for Living and Learning,* and *India: A Light Within* (a collaborative project). She was awarded a Zell Fellowship (MFA program), the Michael R. Gutterman award for poetry, and the Elsie Choy Lee Scholarship (Center for the Education of Women) from the University of Michigan.

She teaches creative writing workshops in Ann Arbor, Michigan, and is a freelance editor, a manuscript coach, and a mentor to her students. *www.zilkajoseph.com*

Acknowledgements

Grateful acknowledgement is made to the editors of the following journals and anthologies in which these poems, some in different versions, first appeared: *Beltway Poetry Review, COG Literary Journal, Dragonfly, Frontier Poetry, Paterson Literary Review, Poetry, Pratik, The Punch Magazine, Quiddity, Review Americana, Sipay* (Seychelles), *The MacGuffin, Repast, the journal of Food* (Ann Arbor Culinary Historians), *The Big Scream.*

"The Suburban Car Dealership Shuttle Driver" was exhibited as part of the Asian American Artist Association (San Francisco) juried event "quest for space," held in the Soma Arts Gallery, San Francisco. A very early version was read on NPR as part of Allison Downey's *Living Room* program.

"God of the Great Blue Window," inspired by a photograph by Chris G.P. , appeared in the book *My Vision, Your Voice: An Artistic Duet*, 2013, a collaborative project involving photography by special needs students and poetry by Michigan poets, edited by Suzanne Scarfone and published by the Macomb Oakland Recreational Center.

"Guests Who Came to Dinner" was a finalist in the Frontier Summer Poetry Contest.

Several of the poems in this book were part of *Lands I Live In*, a chapbook published by Mayapple Press, nominated for a PEN America Beyond Margins award.

"Introduction to Circles" won the Editor's Prize from the *Paterson Literary Review.*

"Mama, Who'd Have Thought" was published in *Sparrows and Dust*, published by the Ridgeway Press. It will appear in *The Poetry Society of Michigan Anthology 2021.*

Notes:

"English as She Is Spoke," Page 48
Pedro Carolino wrote this book to help Portuguese students understand the challenges of learning English. It seems Carolino knew very little English, and had no Portuguese-English dictionary at hand. He consulted a Portuguese–French phrasebook, then a French-English dictionary. This led to some hilarious results. Sadly, his work today is used as an example of botched English usage, and translation disasters.

"Herstory," Page 61
There are many theories about the origins of the Bene Israel, (called "Shanwar Telis" or Saturday oil pressers) from India. The three most well-known theories are (1) they arrived after the destruction of temple by the Romans in 70 C.E.; (2) that they were the descendants of the Lost Tribes, who came around the time of King Solomon in the tenth century B.C.E.; and probably the most popular is that they were fleeing from Galilee and the rule of the Greek overlord Antiochus Epiphanes, in 175 B.C.E. Some scholars seem to think it more likely that they came in the fifth or sixth century C.E. from Yemen or South Arabia or Persia. Sources: *The Jews of India* by Benjamin J. Israel (Mosaic Books), and *The Bene Israel of India: Some Studies* by Benjamin J. Israel (Orient Longman).

"Freedom Song with Ginsberg, Dylan and Marley," Page 83
Fragments of lines or lyrics taken from Allen Ginsberg's poem "America"; from Bob Dylan's song "The Times They Are a Changin'," and "Master's of War": and Bob Marley's "Redemption Song".

"Whose Voices Were Heard," Page 85
Fragments of lines or lyrics from Richard Lovelace, Rudyard Kipling, Jesus Christ Super Star (the musical), Romeo and Juliet (the film), Martin Luther King, Bankim Chandra Chatterjee, Mavis Staples, Rabindranath Tagore, John Milton, Gwendolyn Brooks, Marvin Gaye, Maya Angelou, Bob Marley, the Vedas, the Bible, the Kabbalah, Joy Harjo, African American spirituals, Motown songs and nursery rhymes.

Page 91
m'pnei tikkun ha-olam—Hebrew, before/in the face of the repair of the world.
          —From the Lurianic *Kabbalah.*

Page 91

Tamaso ma jyotir gamaya

From falsehood lead me to truth, (or from the unreal lead me to the real),
From darkness lead me to light,
From death lead me to immortality.
　　　　　—From *The Brihadaranyaka Upanishad*

Significant Laws passed by the English to impose English Literature and Language on the natives of India:

The Charter Act of 1813

The passing of the Charter Act of 1813, the British assumed more responsibility on education in India and relaxed controls on Christian missionary education. Natives were to be introduced to "useful knowledge, and of religious and moral improvement." "Natives must willingly submit from a conviction that we are more wise, more just, more humane, more anxious to improve their condition than any other rulers they could possibly have,"Minute, J. Farish, Bombay Presidency 1813. This lead to the institutionalized study of English Literature. (In contrast, in England, it was only in 1871 that the study of English Literature began at Oxford and Cambridge, as before that only Latin and Greek were studied). Ultimately, this forced study of English Literature lead to the English Education Act of 1835 where the English language was officially made the medium of instruction in education. But English was already being taught for the past 20 years, and this Act allowed them to enforce the language on the natives, made it impossible to be employed unless they learned English, and Indians who applied for public office had to be well-versed in European literature.

Extracts from *Macaulay's Minute*, February 2, 1835

[8] …the dialects commonly spoken among the natives of this part of India contain neither literary nor scientific information, and are moreover so poor and rude that, until they are enriched from some other quarter, it will not be easy to translate any valuable work into them.
[9] What then shall that language be? One-half of the committee maintain that it should be the English. The other half strongly recommend the Arabic and Sanscrit. The whole question seems to me to be—which language is the best worth knowing?

100

[10] …I have never found one among them who could deny that a single shelf of a good European library was worth the whole native literature of India and Arabia. The intrinsic superiority of the Western literature is indeed fully admitted by those members of the committee who support the oriental plan of education.

[11] …It will hardly be disputed, I suppose, that the department of literature in which the Eastern writers stand highest is poetry. And I certainly never met with any orientalist who ventured to maintain that the Arabic and Sanscrit poetry could be compared to that of the great European nations. But when we pass from works of imagination to works in which facts are recorded and general principles investigated, the superiority of the Europeans becomes absolutely immeasurable. **It is, I believe, no exaggeration to say that all the historical information which has been collected from all the books written in the Sanscrit language is less valuable than what may be found in the most paltry abridgments used at preparatory schools in England.** [emphasis added]

[32] It is taken for granted by the advocates of oriental learning that no native of this country can possibly attain more than a mere smattering of English. We know that foreigners of all nations do learn our language sufficiently to have access to all the most abstruse knowledge which it contains sufficiently to relish even the more delicate graces of our most idiomatic writers. There are in this very town natives who are quite competent to discuss political or scientific questions with fluency and precision in the English language. I have heard the very question on which I am now writing discussed by native gentlemen with a liberality and an intelligence which would do credit to any member of the Committee of Public Instruction. Indeed it is unusual to find, even in the literary circles of the Continent, any foreigner who can express himself in English with so much facility and correctness as we find in many Hindoos. Nobody, I suppose, will contend that English is so difficult to a Hindoo as Greek to an Englishman. Yet an intelligent English youth, in a much smaller number of years than our unfortunate pupils pass at the Sanscrit College, becomes able to read, to enjoy, and even to imitate not unhappily the compositions of the best Greek authors. Less than half the time which enables an English youth to read Herodotus and Sophocles ought to enable a Hindoo to read Hume and Milton.

Source: *http://www.mssu.edu/projectsouthasia/history/primarydocs/education/Macaulay001.htm*
From: *Bureau of Education. Selections from Educational Records, Part I (1781-1839).*
Edited by H. Sharp. Calcutta: Superintendent, Government Printing, 1920. Reprint. Delhi: National Archives of India, 1965, 107-117.

Recent Titles from Mayapple Press

Ricardo Jesús Mejías Hernández, tr. Don Cellini, *Libro de Percances/ Book of Mishaps*, 2021
>Paper, 56pp, $18.95 plus s&h
>ISBNÑ 978'952781-05-6

Eleanor Lerman, *Watkins Glen*, 2021
>Paper, 218pp, $22.95 plus s&h
>ISBN: 978-1-952781-01-8

Betsy Johnson, *when animals are animals*, 2021
>Paper, 58pp, $17.95 plus s&h
>ISBN: 978-1-952781-02-5

Judith Kunst, *The Way Through*, 2020
>Paper, 76pp, $17.95 plus s&h
>ISBN: 978-1-936419-98-2

Ellen Stone, *What Is in the Blood*, 2020
>Paper, 72pp, $17.95 plus s&h
>ISBN 978-1-936419-95-1

Terry Blackhawk, *One Less River*, 2019
>Paper, 78pp, $16.95 plus s&h
>ISBN 978-1-936419-89-0

Ellen Cole, *Notes from the Dry Country*, 2019
>Paper, 88pp, $16.95 plus s&h
>ISBN 978-1-936419-87-6

Monica Wendel, *English Kills and other poems*, 2018
>Paper, 70pp, $15.95 plus s&h
>ISBN 978-1-936419-84-5

Charles Rafferty, *Something an Atheist Might Bring Up at a Cocktail Party*, 2018
>Paper, 40pp, $14.95 plus s&h
>ISBN 978-1-936419-83-8

David Lunde, *Absolute Zero*, 2018
>Paper, 82pp, $16.95 plus s&h
>ISBN 978-1-936419-80-7

For a complete catalog of Mayapple Press publications, please visit our website at *www.mayapplepress.com*. Books can be ordered direct from our website with secure on-line payment using PayPal, or by mail (check or money order). Or order through your local bookseller.

In this rich collection of poems, Zilka Joseph takes us on a voyage from her birthplace in India to her immigration to and life in the United States. Even as the airplane from India prepares to land, she thinks "of Dante's *Purgatorio*— / the tiered stages, the tortured souls," foreshadowing the coiling incidents of tokenism and racism, both virulent and "casual," she will encounter in this new land, where "Garam masala is a buzzword," and "Turmeric capsules are a rage." Her poems remember their way back through India's colonial history and the losses of culture, religion, and language which throb into her present tense. Joseph makes use of a number of approaches to form in this collection, ending with a collage of mythic, literary, musical, and historical influences which bring her worlds together into a vision of "dancing in the sun / in our own shining skin / in our beautiful bones." These are brave and beautiful poems.

—Diane Seuss, Author of *frank: sonnets, Still Life with Two Dead Peacocks and a Girl,* and *Four-Legged Girl*

Following the literary tradition of Carolyn Forché and Claudia Rankine, poet Zilka Joseph spins the jarring, interpersonal experience of racism and colonialism into consciousness-exploding verse. In the process, the reader becomes the witness: a terrified, white child gawking at your brown face; a neighbor filing a complaint about the smell of your food cooking; the moment at a dinner party when you become the explainer for your people; encountering ignorance so blatant it leaves you speechless. You can't pore over *In Our Beautiful Bones* and not be transformed by the powerful, emotional landscape of this collection.

—Desiree Cooper, Pulitzer-nominated journalist, and award-winning author of *Know the Mother*

In Our Beautiful Bones reckons with the violence of white supremacy and colonialism. In these poems, Zilka Joseph surveys the ecological, physical, emotional, and psychological traumas of that violence, with a central focus on the agonies of constant interpellation by whiteness's gaze. "O even in Hades salvation is not free," Joseph writes, and we, Joseph makes clear, are in Hades. What should we do? Do we sing songs of praise, even for that which hurts us? Do we smile, as we've been taught? What do we hold onto with our bruised-knuckle hands, especially when we're held apart from each other by prejudice, by distance, by disease? These are the questions *In Our Beautiful Bones* inhabits and wrestles with, all the while hoping to make it through to some place where it would make sense to say "when I say love I mean you / when I say home I mean you."

—Sumita Chakraborty, author of *Arrow* and *Grave Dangers: Poetics and the Ethics of Death in the Anthropocene* (forthcoming)

In *In Our Beautiful Bones,* the poet Zilka Joseph creates a powerful, stunning portrait of life and education in India followed by her journey to America and her effort to assimilate without losing so much that her own culture gave her. She recognizes herself always as a stranger slightly on the outside because her accent, her food, her beliefs are not quite acceptable in suburban America. This is a beautiful book about courage and survival.
—Maria Mazzioti Gillan, American Book Award winner

Zilka Joseph's *In Our Beautiful Bones* samples a wide swath of cultural characters with their gods, heroes, literature, music, and politics as a way to reveal a coherent and poetic story of humanity in all its glorious goodness and heinousness. Let's just say she sucks the marrow and spits it out, letting good and evil, joy and depression, peace and war fall wherever and however. With her mastery of various language rhythms and her clear immigrant eyes, we discover we are all one, no matter the differences of time and space, food, music or politics. Yes, food. We even find her cooking for John Lewis preparatory to making some "good trouble." And this collection is absolutely solid, deep trouble, the kind that connects us in surprising, beautiful and powerful ways that gird us for a mighty fight.
—Lolita Hernandez, author of *Autopsy of an Engine and Other Stories from the Cadillac Plant* and *Making Callaloo in Detroit*

Anyone who has ever been asked, "but where are you really from?" will recognize themselves in Zilka Joseph's *In Our Beautiful Bones.* Aggressions large and small—from colonial decrees and communal violence to sly slurs, innuendo and subtle gestures in a parking lot—populate the lines of these poems, leaving both speaker and reader to decode the languages of inclusion and exclusion spoken so fluently in our nation. What music can be made of otherness? And at what cost? Joseph's gripping poems sing a melody of fury, tenderness and grief that arises from loving a country that doesn't always love you back.
—Kirun Kapur, author of *Women in the Waiting Room,* finalist for the National Poetry Series